T0065368

From Make-Believe Love To Real Love

Resilient Butterfly

authorHOUSE®

AuthorHouse™
1663 Liberty Drive
Bloomington, IN 47403
www.authorhouse.com
Phone: 833-262-8899

Published by AuthorHouse 11/12/2020

ISBN: 978-1-6655-0735-6 (sc)
ISBN: 978-1-6655-0752-3 (e)

Print information available on the last page.

This book is printed on acid-free paper.

CONTENTS

ACKNOWLEDGEMENTS

First and foremost, I would like to thank my lord and savior Jesus Christ for helping get through all the bumps in the road throughout my love life. I know without you I would not have been able to make it this far. I also know that my prayers and my intuition helped me along my love journey.

I would also like to thank my beautiful and talented sister Sunshine who is author, poet, etc. Thank you for always being there for me no matter what the circumstances are. You are truly a blessing from God.

I would also like to thank my big sister Violet for always being supportive of anything I would like to accomplish in life. Thank you for picking me to be your lil sistah.

I would like to thank my cousins Songbird, Tweety Bird, and Barbie for always being there for me throughout the years. Thank you for listening to all my crazy stories. I really appreciate all the love and support you all have shown me it really means a lot to me.

I would also like to thank my Auntie Blue and Auntie Rosa for always being there for me. Thank you for always giving me honest advice.

I would like to thank my God Mom Flora for being such a great Godmother to me. Thank you for always being so genuine and positive.

I would like to thank my loving boyfriend. Thank you for coming into my life and making my life better when it was upside down. Thank you for protecting me and making me feel safe. Thank you for always being so open and nonjudgmental with me. Thanks for always listening to my thoughts, dreams, and goals in life. Thank you for loving me inside and out with all my flaws. Thank you for not only believing in me but supporting me.

DEDICATION

I would like to dedicate this book to anyone who is or has been experiencing challenges with their love life whether you are a teenager or an adult.

My goal is to help motivate you all to not be scared to break bad cycles in relationships that are not good for you. But instead to learn to create healthy cycles in relationships that are good for you.

I believe once you learn to love yourself, you will be able to create healthy relationships. Then, your life will fall into place where you want it to be. Whether your focus is on your career, business, love life, family, etc.

MY INSPIRATIONS FOR THIS BOOK

One of the things that sparked my interest to write this book was another book called "The Man God Has For You" by Stephan Labossiere. I read his book in one day. I was fascinated by how easy it was for me to read it. He made it easy for me to see all the mistakes I had made in my past relationships.

I was able to see clearly why I kept making the same mistakes over and over. I was also able to see how far I have come and what I still need to work on.

The second thing that sparked my interest to write this book was my desire to tell about my past struggles. I wanted to share this information to hopefully prevent other people from making the same mistakes I made. I have learned numerous times to stop giving my valuable time to people who did not deserve it.

No matter what I would do to prove my worth to them, it was never good enough. I have realized that trying to make them see my value was never my job to do in the first place. I realized God was teaching me lessons along the way. It was up to me to put my foot down and realize how precious I am. And I needed to know I deserve the upmost respect. And that if I could not receive it from a person then it was not meant to be.

I needed to do some soul searching for the love I once had for myself.

And once I found it, I needed to hold onto it and never let it go. That is what my most valued treasure was and nobody could take that away from me. Once I found that love for myself, I did not stand for any lack of respect, lack of commitment, lack of loyalty, and so on.

DISCLAIMER

The stories in this book are real however the names of the people involved have been changed to fake names to protect their privacy.

CHAPTER 1

Looks Are Deceiving

My first love James was a cool street cat. He was very charming and funny. All the ladies in the hood used to crush on him. I guess you could say it was something about his eyes and his swag that caught the ladies' attention. James was a real good smooth talker.

We seemed to have a natural chemistry that drew us towards each other. However, timing was never right for us to be together. Until one day we just could not resist each other anymore. That very same day we lost our virginity to each other.

He was in a relationship with my preschool friend Rose. I did not realize it was wrong because I was in love with him. I became even more in love with him after that day. Here I was, not a virgin anymore, in love with someone who was already in a relationship.

Here I was thinking he would leave her for me. He ended up staying with her for quite some time. But he still had feelings for me while he was with her. After that, we never really had the chance to be together.

Now when I think back to that time, I realize I should have never given up my virginity like that. I also realize that I should not have done that to my friend Rose. I would like to apologize to my preschool friend Rose. I never meant to hurt you. I got caught up in the moment and in my feelings. I am terribly sorry for hurting you, that was never my intention.

I do not really want to say I regret giving it up to James. But I do regret the way that it happened. This is something I will have to live with for the rest of my life. I know some of you may be wondering why I did not say I regret losing my virginity in general. To be honest, nobody would have been worth it to lose it to except my boyfriend that I have now. And hell, I am 32 years old now.

I want to share the lessons I learned from this relationship. I learned not to get caught up with someone that is already in a relationship. I learned not to forget about my morals and values while seeking love. I learned not to let my standards down.

I also learned from this relationship that you should not always take a risk because I took the risk and it cost me a friendship.

Zodiac sign: Capricorn

Questions I wish someone would have asked me

1. Why are you pursuing a man that is unavailable?

2. Why are drawn to a street man?

3. Why would you allow yourself to fall in love with a man that loves the street life?

4. Why is your main focus on boys instead of school?

5. Why did you feel the need to lose your innocence at an early age?

6. Why are you looking for love at such a young age?

7. Why are your emotions running you wild?

Love Is Blind

My first heartache started at the age of 15 ½. I met this man named Jim. I had been crushing on Jim for quite some time. Finally, one day I was at a liquor store. And one of my high school friends Kayla told him that I had a crush on him right in front of me. I could not believe she did that. At that moment, I was not ready to tell him yet.

The reason I was too shy to say anything to him is because I was 5 or 6 years younger than him. But it turned out that we were both feeling each other so we decided to give it a chance. We started off as friends and then became girlfriend and boyfriend over time.

Things moved very quickly with us. Before we made it to 6 months, I had already met a lot of his family members. I was so happy because family is especially important to me. After a while, I would start to see the mind games he was playing with me. Jim would ask me for money to get high and party with.

I was never taught as a child to never give money to a man. So often I would give up my allowance money and some of my paycheck to him. I was so young and naïve thinking he was so in love with me. I thought the love, affection, and money would keep him happy.

I was sadly mistaken. He would accuse me from time to time of cheating on him. But hell, he was the one cheating on me. I found out twice that he was stepping out on me but I still stayed.

I also still remember that I had a sweet sixteen birthday party that Jim was supposed to attend but did not show up until the party was over. And my heart ended up broken once again.

My breaking point for our relationship was when I moved to a different city. I remember asking him to go to prom with me and he said he would. But as my prom got closer, he became less available and it was hard to reach him. He finally ended up telling me he was not going to be able to go.

I was so heartbroken and devastated that I had no prom date. I knew from that point on that the love I had for him was stronger than the love he had from me.

I want to share the lessons I learned from this relationship. I learned if the communication, love, and trust is not there in the beginning then it will not work in the long run. I also learned being with a man that does not share at least most of the same values and morals you have will not work. Being with a man that does believe in God the way you do will not work.

Zodiac sign: Pisces

Questions I wish someone would have asked me

1. Why is this man's love so precious to you verses your love for yourself?

2. Why do you value this man more than you value yourself?

3. Why are you attracted to older men that don't have anything going for themselves?

4. Why do you feel the need to stay with a man that does not value himself?

5. Why do you feel the need to fix a man that's not willing to fix his self?

6. Why do you feel sorry for a man that doesn't feel sorry for himself?

7. Why do you help a man financially that's not willing to help himself?

8. Why do you stay with a man that accuses you of stuff you haven't done?

9. Why do you stay with a man that mentally abuses you?

10. Why do you continue to stay with a man that tears you down instead of lifting you up?

Do Not Let the Pretty Eyes Fool You

Here I was 18 years old with another guy who was older than me. Desmond was handsome with sexy eyes. He was a real street cat. He was also a smooth talker. I feel in love with him very quickly.

Desmond spent as little time as possible with me. I do not recall us ever spending the night together. I thought he would be different from my previous ex. But he was no different. He wanted money from me too. I would work so hard as a cashier at a fast-food restaurant just to give most of my money to him.

I never even got to see where the money I was giving him was going. I just felt sorry for him and wanted to help him.

I remember two instances when he stole from me. First, I got a new phone and he stole that from me. Second, I left my purse on the bed and he stole all my money out of my wallet. After that, I ended things because all he was doing was tearing me down.

He was not helping me. He was taking away from me. I knew I would never get ahead in life if I stayed with him. Therefore, I decided it would be my best interest to walk away.

I want to share the lessons I learned from this relationship. First, I learned to not be with someone that does not listen to my feelings. Secondly, I learned to not be with someone that does not respect me. Third, I learned to not be with someone I cannot trust.

Fourth, I learned not to be with someone with different morals and values. Fifth, I learned not to be with someone who steals from me. Sixth, I learned not to be with someone that brings me down. Then, last but not least, I learned not to be with a manipulator since no good will come from it.

Zodiac sign: Leo

Questions I wish someone would have asked me

1. Why are you attracted to men that play mind games?

2. Why do you give your valuable time to disloyal men?

3. Why do you stay with a man that mentally abuses you?

4. Why do you stay with a man that can't give you what you want?

5. Why do you stay with a man you can't trust?

6. Why do you stay with a man that doesn't respect you?

7. Why do you stay with a man that has no morals?

8. Why do you help a man get ahead in life that's not willing to help himself?

9. Why do you trust a man that never gave you a reason to trust him?

10. Why do you stay with a man that doesn't care about your goals in life?

Lost In His Charm

When I was 18 or 19, I had this boyfriend name Tariq. He was well known in the city I was living in. We first met in the drive thru at a fast-food restaurant and he asked me out on a date. After our first date, we continued to date and eventually got into a relationship. He was handsome and funny. He was also an incredibly talented underground rapper.

There were two things I noticed different about him from my last ex. He gave me certain qualities I wanted like faithfulness, quality time, and affection. But unfortunately, he wanted money from me as well like my exes. I could not understand why he needed money from me.

Especially since he was supposedly pimping. I felt he should not have been asking me for anything. Maybe he was not really pimping the way he said he was. I never really knew what he was doing with the money I was giving him.

I knew he had a daughter so I figured he was giving the money to her. Tariq was not a big partier or anything. He really was interested in becoming a big rapper. We broke up one day because I felt I could not trust him anymore. One day he stopped calling and I discovered he went to jail. After that moment, I knew it was best for me to move on.

I want to share the lessons I learned from this relationship. I learned to not be with a man that I did not trust. Also, I learned I should not be with a man that did not respect women.

Zodiac sign: Taurus

Questions I wish someone would have asked me

1. Why are you attracted to men that live that fast life?

2. Why do you feel obligated to help a man get ahead in life?

3. Why do you stay with a man that does not value women?

4. Why do you give your time to a man that can't help you get ahead in life?

5. Why do you give your hard-earned money to a man that doesn't deserve it?

The Family Man

When I was 20 years old, I had this boyfriend named Derek. He was nice looking but he was not a one woman man. However, by the time I figured that out I was already in love. He was dating one of my good friends from high school. And I did not find that out until I was already in love with him.

He was wrong on so many levels. I could not believe I was in a position where I had to pick between my friend and the man I was in love with. I was so torn on what to do. I had made the decision to stay with him. I lived with him and a few of his family members for a few years.

During that time, I started to discover his deceitful cheating ways. I know two times for sure that he cheated on me. I also discovered his temper and the fact that he did not have respect for his mother. I did not like it at all. I should have walked away.

The reason I decided to stay was because I felt so connected to him and his family. I loved him and them. And he loved me too to a certain extent. I met the majority of all his family. He gave me a lot of affection and quality time. But he just lived the life of a Rockstar. I guess he could not help his self.

One day we felt like things were going to get better in our relationship. So, we decided to get a place of our own together. I believed in my heart that once we moved away into our own place that he would stop cheating on me. Unfortunately, that was not the case. He ended up cheating again later down the line. I was so shocked and in disbelief that I was going through this again.

I strongly believed he was cheating with the neighbor downstairs. My intuition was telling me he was. I could not catch him but I felt it in my spirit. I remember asking myself why does he feel the need to cheat on me. I knew I had all the qualities any man would dream to have in a partner.

The next time he cheated on me was a time when I went with him to a family game night. He left me that whole day to be with another women in the apartments we were at.

I did not figure that out till later on that evening. I remember feeling lonely and foolish for coming to the party just to get left by him. I remember playing basketball with his niece and nephew to pass time.

Later I would discover with them what Derek was really up to that day. We ended up going around the back of the apartment complex when suddenly God told me to look up. When I looked up, I saw my man kissing a pregnant woman.

I was so angry and heartbroken. I remember telling his sister what happened. And I remember some family members laughing and I felt humiliated. I just wanted to go home after that.

After that I kept saying to myself why did he invite me here if he knew his intentions were ill from the beginning. I guess God needed to let me see this with my own eyes. God wanted me to see that he was not going to change.

I remember the last straw for me was when a random girl was in our place. I asked her who was she here for and she said my man's name. I said oh really that is my man and I told her that she needed to leave my place.

I could not believe he was going to have sex or oral sex with her in our bedroom while I was in the shower. I was so upset. I could not believe him. That was my final deal breaker. I remember him and I got into it that day. Verbally and physically.

I remember crying and praying to God to get me out of the situation I was in. I was not in a good space. I was not in a healthy relationship.

I was not happy. God answered my prayer and I moved with two of my Aunts. I am so grateful and blessed I was able to get out of that situation. My life changed for the better after that day.

I remember not dating for a long time. I decided to take a break from romantic relationships. So that I could work on my relationship with God and my goals in life. Once I focused on those things my life started to get in line.

I want to share the lessons I learned from this relationship. I learned to not continue a relationship with a man that does not respect his mother. I learned to not continue a relationship with a man that does not respect me. I learned to not be with a man that did not respect his family.

Zodiac sign: Taurus

Questions I wish someone would have asked me

1. Why do you stay with a man that doesn't respect his mother?

2. Why do you stay with a man that doesn't respect your friends and family?

3. Why do you stay with a man that verbally and physically abuses you?

4. Why do you stay with a man that does not value you?

5. Why do you stay with a cheating man?

6. Why do you stay with a man that lacks morals?

CHAPTER

6

Blinded By Sex

W
hen I was 24, I dated this street cat name Raheem. We meet off of the dating website Mocospace. We dated for a while before we made it official. What drew me to him was his swag and his looks. He was also mad funny.

We really did not have anything in common except sex chemistry. We lacked emotions, communication, spirituality, and trust in our relationship.

During the time me and Raheem dated off and on, I never got to meet his family. It was not until way later down the line that I got to speak to his mom and see her in person. And that was only because he had got locked up and wanted me to hold him down. I was so into him that I would help him out financially a lot.

I remember feeling lost and helpless so many days and nights. I was wondering why the simple things I wanted from him were not coming together. It took me a while to realize that he was a straight manipulator.

I realized all he cared about was his name in the streets. How he needed to stay up to date with his cars by having big flashy rims. He wanted to have gold teeth, jewelry, hoes, weed, and money.

One day I woke up and asked myself why am I helping this man get this stuff. Especially since all I am getting in return is good sex, heartache, and anger. So, I decided I did not want to be with him anymore since I could not get simple things in return. It was a good decision I made for myself.

I want to share the lessons I learned from this relationship. I learned to never get caught up in a relationship with a manipulator because it will be hard to walk away. I learned to never invest my feelings into a man that put his feelings for the streets before me.

I learned that I need to stop giving my hard-earned money to men that don't deserve it. I learned to never give my time to a man that could not give me the qualities God says I deserve.

Zodiac sign: Gemini

Questions I wish someone would have asked me

1. Why are you attracted to fuck boys?

2. Why do you continue to date a man that won't bring you around his family?

3. Why do you continue the relationship when it lacks respect, love, and trust?

4. Why do you stay with a man that can't do anything for you but bring you down?

5. Why do you stay with a man that still thinks like a boy?

6. Why do you stay with a man only worried about material things?

7. Why do you stay with a man that doesn't see no wrong in what they do?

8. Why do you continue to date a man with no goals?

9. Why do continue to date a man that's not humble?

CHAPTER

7

Trust Your Instincts

When I was 28 years old, I met this man named Jaden. Me and Jaden met at a Bart station and it was a beautiful day that day. I remember looking at him and thinking that he was probably a bad boy. But I decided to ignore my intuition because Jaden was good looking and his swag was on 10.

I could not get enough of Jaden. Unfortunately, I ran into the same problems I had with my last ex. We did not share any of the same values or morals. We only had sex chemistry.

I remember asking him are we official and his response was "I think so". I should have known then that he just wanted to be friends with benefits. I never really thought about his response. I was just cool with it.

I remember when we got to six months I was ready to meet his mom and some of his family members. I was able to meet his son very briefly and I met one of his cousins. However, I never got to meet his mom, dad, or other family members.

I felt like he was hiding something from me because we never really spent the amount of quality time I wanted us to. He barely even spent the night with me. Some days were better than others. We never really talked or texted that much. He told me he was more of a in person type of guy.

I remember one day noticing a gold ban on his left hand. I asked him if he was married or engaged, he said no. I believed him and we continued our relationship. I never saw that gold ban again.

I really loved Jaden even though he was not giving me all the things I wanted and needed. I guess I was content with the little effort he put forth and the good sex he had to offer me.

There were a couple times my intuition told me that this man was going to hurt me but I kept ignoring the signs. In the beginning of our relationship, Jaden never asked me for money.

It was not until we reached six months that he started to ask for little money here and there. It was mainly supposed to be used to help him out with his son. However, later on, I found out that he was saving up the money he was getting from me so that he could go on a trip to Hawaii.

The day he went on his vacation to Hawaii, was the same day he told me that he was spending time with his cousin. He sent me a photo of himself and not one with him and his cousin. So, I asked him to send me a picture of them both together and he could not.

He immediately got very defensive. I knew something was up then. I never talked to him after that day. I waited like a week or two and ended up calling his phone. His fiancé answered the phone and said he could not come to the phone. I ended up finding out through social media he ended up dying from a stroke. I was so sad when I found out he passed. I could not believe it.

It took me awhile to want to date or get into a relationship again. I was tired of running into men that were immature and unavailable.

I want to share the lessons I learned from this relationship. I learned to never date a pretty boy because he probably has a woman or a couple women hiding somewhere. I learned to never continue a relationship with a man that does not meet my standards. Also, I learned that I shouldn't continue to date a man that was not that into me.

Zodiac sign: Scorpio

Questions I wish someone would have asked me

1. Why are you attracted to good looking bad boys?

2. Why do you feel obligated to take care of a man financially?

3. Why do you stay with a man you know you can't trust?

4. Why do you stay with a man that believes his own lies?

5. Why do you stay with a man that can't give you a clear answer about your status?

6. Why do you stay with a man that doesn't hold the same values and morals you hold?

8

Red Flags Are Your Friend

When I was 30 years old, I met a man named Derrick. It was a cold gloomy day. I was walking to a Bart station and he stopped me. He pulled over and parked and got out to talk to me.

I was in a happy place in my life and I was not in a place where I wanted to waste any more of my time. I let that be known from the jump. I told him a list of things I was not going for.

He said okay to my list and told me to take down his number. He also told me that he wanted to take me to lunch one day. It took me a minute to text or call him because I was not quite sure if I trusted that he would not waste my time. I decided in the meantime to date people on a dating site until I was sure.

One day we did start talking and we planned our first date. Our first date was interesting. He wanted to sit next to me while we ate our food instead of sitting across from each other.

This was different for me. I did not understand why he was doing that until I talked to one of my God brothers. I was happy to hear the reason why. Apparently, when someone wants to sit next to you instead of across from you it is a sign that they trust you.

I really liked Derrick. He was good looking and he had swag. We went on many of dates before we became a couple. I remember asking him if we were official now and he said "I think so".

His answer should have rung a bell in my head that he was not looking for a commitment. I should have known then he just wanted to be friends with benefits. I never really thought about his response. I just rolled with it. It was not till after some time that I started to notice little red flags.

One time, I was in the car with him and I was trying to connect my Bluetooth to his car. I ended up seeing other women names. I remember I got upset about that. He tried to cover it up and be slick but I had already saw it. I believe I confronted him that same day and I cannot remember what lie he told me about it.

Next, I started to trip on how he only had a certain amount of time for me. And how he could never really spend the night. We never spent the holidays together. I could not even go see him coach his basketball team. Also, he never let me meet his immediate family except his mom.

We never went to family events together. I remember being so puzzled why he could not give me the things that I wanted and needed. I finally figured it out later down the line.

Even though he could not give all the things I desired from him in general he did treat me good. That is why there is no love lost. I just took it as a lesson learned. I know you are probably wondering how he was good to me when he lied to me. Let me explain.

The reason I say he was good to me is because he took me on dates all the time. And every single time, he payed for the date and our food. He also took me to school sometimes. He gave me money for pretty much whatever I needed and he helped pay for my behind the wheel driver lessons. He just was not available to give me the time I wanted and needed.

It took me some time to put everything together. Time to figure out why things were not adding up. He had lied to me about having kids. He lied to me about him living with his baby mother. He lied to me about him being married. He lied to me about his age. And only God knows what else.

Now that I look back, I know why he hid all those things from me. He knew I would have never given him a chance if he would have told me the truth. I hate that I kept the relationship going on as long as I did. Especially after I knew what was going on. I am glad I eventually listened to my intuition and let it go.

I guess what kept me with Derrek was our sex chemistry and what he was doing for me financially. He gave me things no man had ever given me before. So, I appreciated what he had to give because I was not used to getting that. Derrek never ever asked me for money and I loved that. I was just so happy I had finally broken that cycle.

I learned a lot about myself from this relationship. I knew what I needed to do next to prevent any of the former bad things from recurring to me ever again.

I decided to start reading books to learn my value.

I decided to read "The Power Of The Pussy" by Kara King and "The Wait" by Devon Franklin and Meagan Good. I learned so much of what I should and should not have been doing while I was in my past relationships.

I also decided to journal about all the things I could offer a man and about all the things I wanted from a man. Once I did that, it didn't take long for my wishes to come true.

I want to share the lessons I learned from this relationship. First, never stay with a man that believes his own lies. Second, never be with a man that is unavailable to give you what your heart desires. Third, never put your trust in a man that never gives you a reason to trust.

Zodiac sign: Cancer

Questions I wish someone would have asked me

1. Why do you fall in love so easily?

2. Why do you ignore the red flags that are in your face?

3. Why do you ignore your instincts?

4. Why do you put so much faith in a relationship that has been broken by trust?

5. Why do you stay with a man that you know you are not destined to be with?

6. Why do you continue to stay with a man that doesn't show you off to the world?

7. Why do you continue to stay with a man that breaks your heart?

8. Why do you feel the need to stay with a man that doesn't meet all of your dream man qualities?

9. Why do you feel the need to stay with a man that doesn't see the good you see in his self?

CHAPTER

9

Ready For Love

A t the age of 31, I was on this dating website called plenty of fish. One day, this man named Anthony reached out to me. He was 10 years older than me. He wrote me a long nice message. I really liked what he said so one day I decided to give him a call.

We had a nice conversation. One thing I really liked about him was his voice. I never talked to any man with a voice like his. His voice sparked excitement into me.

I remember asking him a question while we were on the phone one day. I had asked if he had any kids and he said yes.

Up to that point, I was so used to being hurt by men that had kids. I thought it would be in my best interest to not date another man with kids. So, I was thinking about ending things with Anthony.

Until I talked to my God mother and she told me it will be hard to find an older man with no kids. I took time and really thought about what she said and what my intuition was telling me. I ended up deciding to give him a chance. I am so glad I made that decision.

Anthony is so sweet, handsome, charming, and funny. He has many of the qualities I was looking for in a man. He is so thoughtful. And the way he glances at me while we watch TV together makes my heart melt. He pays attention to me like no man has before. He sure is different from the rest. He is very romantic. He gives me flowers and small gifts just because.

He gives me lots of affection and quality time. He treats me like the queen that I am. I could not be any happier than I am now. He has given me every reason to trust him. He knows all about my heartache and pain from my previous relationships. And he has never done anything to disrespect me.

He gave me a key to his place while we were just dating. I believe we were just dating for a total of 3 months. I could not believe he gave me a key. No man had ever done that before for me. He communicates with me very well.

He can be there for me physically, mentally, emotionally, spiritually, and financially. He respects me, trust me, and loves me. He is patient with me. He admires me. He helps me cook. He helps me level up.

For the first time, I have a man that is available in all the ways I need him to be. And he wants nothing more from me but respect, love, and affection. I give him all of that and more.

After my last relationship, I was almost ready to give up on love and I am glad I did not. I do not know what the future will hold for me and him. But I know I am living in the moment. Taking things one day at a time and loving every bit of it.

Reading, journaling, and praying helped me to grow in all the ways

I needed to. In the end, I was able to gain a man with most of the same values, morals, and beliefs that I have. A man that has not only become my boyfriend but one of my best friends.

Zodiac sign: Gemini

HOW I OVERCAME

To stop the bad relationships cycles, I had to learn how to love, respect, and value myself. I also rekindled my relationship with God. I prayed a lot throughout all the challenges I was facing. I called on Jesus to help me in my time of need.

Whether I was experiencing happiness, sorrow, anger, rage, or fear Jesus gave me all the answers I needed. And for that I am forever grateful. If I did not have a relationship with God, I would not be in the best state like I am now. I have grown so much over the last few years. And I plan to continue growing.

MY ADVICE

If you find yourself dealing with the same problems in relationships, I highly recommend for you to read the books I mentioned in this book and for you to start journaling about what you want in your next relationship.

In the meantime, embrace your past in relationships and be assured that there is somebody out there that can and will give you everything you need. You just have to be patient and ready for it.

From here on out, make sure you pay attention to words and actions when you are in a relationship. If their actions don't match with their words, do yourself a favor and move on. You are destined for greatness and you don't need no one holding you back.

Also, if you have any regular goals you should start taking steps to reach them. Even if it's a small step, every step counts in the end.

ABOUT ME

Resilient Butterfly is a former foster youth. She was born and raised in San Francisco, California. Resilient Butterfly has overcome many obstacles in her life. She is smart, funny, talented, a go getter, God fearing, and optimistic.

Resilient Butterfly spoke to two different audiences about her experience in the foster care system. Resilient Butterfly was a participant in a mentoring program. Resilient Butterfly volunteered for many events that specifically helped the homeless population and she helped an organization that helps to better the foster care system.

Resilient Butterfly recently got her AA in Liberal Arts and Social & Behavioral Science and is currently pursuing her career in nursing. Additionally, she is working on another book, trying to become a fashion model, and planning to launch an online clothing store. Resilient Butterfly hopes to inspire other women to chase after their dreams regardless of the obstacles they may face.

Printed in the United States
By Bookmasters